100% UNOFFICIAL
ROBLOX

BUILD IT, WIN IT!

ISBN 978-1-338-72678-7

10 9 8 7 6 5 4 3 2 1   22 23 24 25 26

Printed in the U.S.A.   40

First edition, February 2022

CONTENTS

IT LOOKS LIKE YOU HAVE A LOT OF EXPLORING TO DO . . . LUCKY YOU!

INTRODUCTION

Welcome to Roblox! Maybe you're a **NEWCOMER** to the platform . . .

Or a **HARDENED VETERAN** . . .

Whether you're looking to just have **FUN PLAYING** . . .

Or to **CREATE GAMES** of **YOUR OWN** . . .

You'll find **TONS** of useful **TIPS, TRICKS,** and **GUIDANCE** in this book!

ORIGINS OF ROBLOX

Roblox is the biggest game-building platform in the world, and it's been going longer than *Minecraft* or *Fortnite*.

2007
Builders Club (later Roblox Premium) is added.

2004
A beta version of the platform is created by David Baszucki and Erik Cassel.

2006
Roblox officially launches.

2013
Developer Exchange launched, which allows creators to convert in-game earnings into real-world cash.

2016
Roblox goes VR with its Oculus Rift edition.

2011
First "Hack Week" held, where developers share innovative concepts for Roblox.

2020
Roblox launches the "Play Together" game sort, to help players in COVID-19 lockdown find social games. Gamers hold lockdown birthday parties on Roblox!

"WE WANT EVERYONE ON ROBLOX TO BUILD THINGS, IN ADDITION TO PLAYING GREAT GAMES!"

David Baszucki, Roblox cofounder

> DRESS YOUR AVATAR IN NATTY CLOTHES, AND THEY COULD LOOK AS COOL AS ME. WELL, MAYBE NOT QUITE THIS COOL!

GETTING STARTED
PERSONAL ACCOUNT

If you don't already have a Roblox account, go to **Roblox.com**, and you'll see the sign-up form. We suggest that you have your parent or guardian with you (see page 12). Ask them for help choosing a password—make sure you can remember it and that no one can guess it. And only enter it when logging in! Roblox will never ask for your password in a chat window or in the middle of a game.

SECRET IDENTITY

For online safety reasons, don't use your real name for your username. If another user has that name already, you can't use it. And if you want to change your name later, it'll cost you Robux (see page 16)!

FACT BOX

Today, Roblox has over 90 million regular players and four million developers!

APPY DAYS

You'll need to download the app to run games: It's available for Windows, iOS, Android, and Xbox One. Sorry, all you PlayStation 4 and Nintendo Switch owners!

FACT BOX

Roblox was initially developed under the name **DynaBlocks**!

MAKING AN AVATAR

You want to look good when you're gaming, right? Of course you do!

GET THE LOOK

Your avatar is how you'll appear in games and what other users will see when you interact with them. So it's no surprise some people spend a lot of time on theirs. If you're not into creating games, this is an easier way to customize Roblox and make it your own.

You can choose to be male or female, adjust body parts, and change your face, hair, clothes, shoes, and accessories. You'll notice a lot of the more interesting options cost Robux!

> T-SHIRT . . . CHECK.
> SHORTS . . . CHECK.
> PLAID SHIRT . . . CHECK!

MAKE YOUR OWN

If you want to get more advanced, it's possible to make your own clothes, upload them to Roblox, put them on your avatar, and even sell them to other users. There's no program within Roblox to do this, but various art programs will do the job—www.jspaint.app is a good free option.

COMMUNITY

There are several ways to get involved with other Roblox users.

FRIENDS

You can send any user a friend request by going on their page. If they accept it, you're friends! You can message them and hang out in a friends-only place. There's a limit of 200 friends per user.

FOLLOWERS

You can also choose to follow another user. This is more like following someone on social media, and it's useful for keeping up with your favorite developers.

TOP TIP!

If you want to create a group, there's a one-time fee of 100 Robux.

TOP TIP!

You can't own, or be a member of, more than 100 groups at once. (Who has time to be involved in 100 groups anyway?)

GROUPS

Groups are mini communities on Roblox. Some bring together players of a particular game or genre of games, or creators with shared interests. Some are used for organizing gaming sessions or just for discussion.

▶ STAY SAFE

A few essential tips for navigating the Roblox world safely . . .

You (or your parent or guardian) may have heard about safety problems with Roblox. But Roblox is safe to play, as long as you're aware of a few things.

WHO'S OUT THERE?

Roblox is played in online spaces with other users. Most of the users are kids—but there are also adult users, including a lot of the creators. So it's a space where kids and adults are interacting, and you can't necessarily tell who's who.

Let your parent or guardian know that you're playing Roblox, and get them to read this part of the book, so that they know what it's about. The main thing they should know is that Roblox is made with kids in mind, and is a great way to learn creativity and take your first steps into game design.

> YOU CAN POLICE THE GAME—MAKE SURE YOU REPORT ANYTHING YOU'RE NOT COMFORTABLE WITH.

> WATCH FOR POLICE-THEMED GAMES!

KEEP CONTROL

When you sign up for Roblox, make sure that you enter your correct age since under-13s get appropriate filtering on the chat function.

Your parent or guardian can get their own login and access the Account Restrictions settings. This login also allows the user to see your recent activity, including messages, creations, and recently played games—and restrict how you communicate with other players. You can also restrict who can find you when they search for other players.

CENSORED

APPROPRIATE MATERIAL

Usually, when you buy or download a game, it has a rating that tells you what age it's appropriate for. Roblox is an E10+—but that's just the rating for the basic software. Anyone can create a game in Roblox and upload it for anyone else to play. The games aren't rated—there just isn't time to look at every obby and battle-arena game that gets uploaded.

The Roblox staff do look at games and check for inappropriate material. But horror, violence, and gory content are allowed on the platform. For instance, a game with blood wouldn't get an E10+ rating, but there are games featuring blood on Roblox.

PLAYING NICE

Be civil to other Roblox users— basically, behave how you'd like them to behave toward you. If another player is annoying you, you can block them. If they're swearing, won't leave you alone when you ask them to, ask you for personal information, or make it difficult for you to play the game, you can report them, too. But don't report someone just because they beat you in a game. Getting someone in trouble when they've done nothing wrong isn't cool.

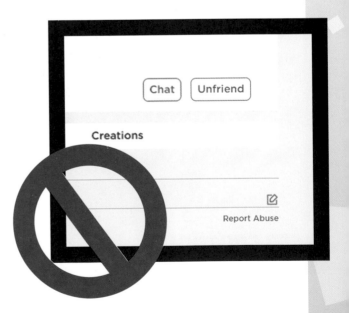

When you report someone, you'll see a selection of categories describing different types of bad behavior. If a user is behaving inappropriately and making you uncomfortable, tell a parent or guardian about it.

Cookie Ears

🔲 75

Heart Face Mask

🔲 25

MONEY GRABBING

Roblox is free to play, but there are in-game purchases that are made with Robux (see page 16). Kids and parents/guardians should talk about this, because it's likely kids will need someone else to pay for the Robux using a credit or debit card. There are controls to restrict how much money a user can spend.

While it is perfectly fine to ask your parents if you are interested in buying Robux, don't take advantage by buying loads of things with their money! You'll be doing them a huge favor.

Horse Face & Fallon

🔲 400

Burger Bunsie

🔲 150

Blue Motherboard

🔲 150

Green Apple Headphones

🔲 25

Toy Animation Pack

🔲 250

ROBUX ___ U
HOW TO $PEND IT!

Beware of those offering free money on Roblox—there's no such thing!

> MONEY DOESN'T GROW ON TREES IN ROBLOX. OR ANYWHERE. YOU HAVE TO BUY IT OR EARN IT!

GETTING ROBUX

Robux is the currency of Roblox. There are four ways to get it:

1 Buy it with regular, real-world money.

2 Sell passes for games you've made.

3 If you're a Roblox Premium member, you can also sell shirts, pants, and access to places—and get a share of the profit!

4 Become a member of Roblox Premium (which also costs real-world money). Members get Robux every month—the amount depends on what tier of membership you have.

TOP TIP!

Changing your username costs a whopping **1,000 Robux**, so think carefully before you choose it!

V. L

28,000

CUTE Red Flannel Crop Top

96

DODGE THE SCAMMERS

There are loads of games that promise you FREE ROBUX and websites that claim to be able to generate Robux for you if you install their apps or watch their videos. Worse still, some of them may try to get personal information out of you in return for Robux. These are all scams—stay far away!

The **only** way to get Robux is to buy them—or to sell things in the game—and only the Roblox company sells them. Anyone else who claims they can sell you Robux away from the Roblox site and apps is lying.

TOP TIP!

You can upload your own audio files for your games, but this also costs Robux, with the cost depending on how long your audio is.

> HAVE YOU SEEN ANYONE ACTING SUSPICIOUSLY AROUND HERE? MAKING ROBLOX OFFERS THAT SEEM TOO GOOD TO BE TRUE? WELL, IF YOU DO, LET ME KNOW . . .

donation c/o
frameworks™
21,248

SO, DO YOU *NEED* ROBUX?

Not necessarily—most of Roblox is free to use. Very few games charge you to play, and in our Top Tens in this book, we'll mostly focus on the free ones. There are in-game purchases that can make games easier, but that depends on whether you want them to be easier.

You can also spend Robux when you redesign your avatar. But again, you can use the free items in the catalog; the games will be just the same!

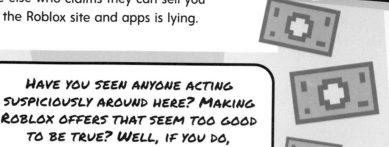

ball dbz
12,800

Boue
6,700

Piggy Head
75

[MD] Medical
Divison
20,000

▶ MAKING TRADES

Roblox Premium users can trade items and Robux with others.

> IT'S NOT AS COMPLICATED AS LIFE ON WALL STREET, BUT MAKE SURE YOU DON'T GET RIPPED OFF!

STRAIGHT SWAP OR ADD ROBUX?

If you want to make a trade, go to that user's profile and select the Trade Items option. Find the items you want to trade. If you feel like they're not equal in value or that the other person needs a little more encouragement to sell, you can throw in some Robux.

However! If you use Robux, then Roblox will pocket a 30% transaction fee—which means that for every 10 Robux spent in a trade, Roblox keeps three. So the value isn't quite as good as just exchanging items. Also, the amount of Robux you offer can't be more than 50% of the value of the original item (after the transaction fee has been subtracted).

Your Inventory · All Accessories · Your Offer

Red Baseball Cap · 441 · Riptide · 298 · Sk9r Boi · 328 · Starry Egg of the Wild Ride · 298

Page 1

Sk9r Boi · 328

Plus Robux amount

Total Value:

Roblox Player's Inventory · All Accessories · Your Request

Portrait of a

Portrait of a Hero in · 313

TOP TIP!

Roblox can't undo a trade after it's gone through, so make sure it's what you want—and don't let other users pressure you into trades!

DODGE THE SCAMMERS PART II

As with Robux, there are users out there who will try to scam you on trades and other types of deals. People might promise real-world money in exchange for items or try to get you to let them use your account—or make a two-stage deal where you have to trust that they'll come back and fulfill the second part. Never go along with these!

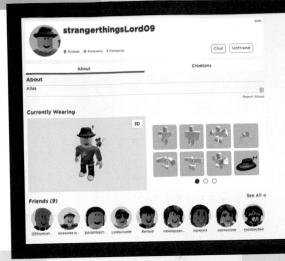

Always make trades within the game itself, and remember—if a trade seems weird or too good to be true, it probably is. And if you see anyone scamming, report them using the **Report Abuse** button.

TOP TIP!

Roblox and the games on it are always being updated. The information in this book is correct at the time of writing—but things change and glitches are fixed!

▶ OBBY GAMES

If you've never played a game on Roblox before, obbys are an ideal place to start. And if you want to make your own games, they're a great place to start, too.

Spend a little time exploring different obbys and how they work, and then try making your own.

▶ THE WORLD OF OBBYS

These are the simplest games in Roblox—but that doesn't mean they're the easiest!

"Obby" might sound like a strange word, but it is short for "obstacle"— these games are obstacle courses. They're also sometimes called parkour games. To win, you need to get past a series of tricky jumps, tightropes, climbing walls, traps, and stuff like that.

There are tons of obby games on Roblox because they're simple to build—the gameplay is really straightforward. The player just has to get from one end to the other—and so lots of designers start by making an obby. This means that obbys can be fairly similar—you often see the same obstacles in a different order.

THERE SHOULD BE NO OBSTACLES TO HAVING FUN!

They're also a good way to get the hang of playing Roblox— the rules and controls are "obby-vious," and although there's usually a leaderboard, you're only really competing with yourself. There are some very clever and imaginative obbys out there—though they might have you pulling your hair out in frustration!

★ WIN IT! | HERE ARE OUR TOP TIPS FOR TACKLING OBBYS...

1 PRECISION

Play on a computer or console instead of a touchscreen. A lot of obbys need very careful movements, otherwise you plummet to your death! Plus, you can be more precise with a keyboard or controller.

2 DON'T RUSH!

Some obbys have a time limit—but even if they do, going too fast is the quickest way to mess it up. Take your time and get it right.

3 AVOID THE CHAT

In this type of game, you don't need distractions!

4 WRAPAROUNDS

Some of the tougher obstacles are known as "wraparounds"—jumps where you must go around a wall. These are a real challenge! If you want to tackle these, there are some handy "wraparound practice" games out there so you can refine your technique.

5 WALLHOPS

Another technique is the "wallhop." Hoppable walls have horizontal stripes. For this, you need to play with a keyboard and have the Shift Lock Switch turned on. Walk up to the wall with the camera positioned above your head, hold Shift and W while jumping, and swish the mouse from side to side. Yes, this takes a little bit of practice—but it enables you to hop up walls!

It's getting hot!

Don't look down!

Wraparound challenge

TOP TEN

OBBYS

Even within this most basic type of Roblox game, there's loads of variety—from puzzles that need to be taken slowly and steadily to mad races against the clock.

10 ESCAPE MCDONALD'S!

It's called fast food for a reason! But plan your moves rather than jumping in without thinking.

It's pretty old now, but this remains a favorite. You progress through a network of McDonald's restaurants, jumping between french fries, dodging spilled sauce, and making your way across a lake of soda. The gameplay is standard obby stuff—platform jumping, finding the safe path, and so on—but the humor of the design lifts it above the crowd. It's very silly and very fun.

★ WIN IT!

To save you time on the annoying Which French Fry? bridge, the safe route is: left path, right path, left path, middle path.

9 PARKOUR

In Parkour, it's a case of jump up, jump up, and get down!

Not one for beginners! This obby, set in a dark urban landscape, is inspired by real-life parkour, requiring you to leap between rooftops, make tricky jumps off posts, and hop across walls. The world of **Parkour** is cool and atmospheric, and the designers have really thought about how to make it challenging. The combo counter is a nice touch—but you'll need to get the hang of some advanced obby techniques before you can tackle this one.

★ WIN IT!

If you need to drop smoothly down the side of a building, try moving very close to the edge, switching to first person, and then holding the Shift key.

8 MINIONS ADVENTURE OBBY: DESPICABLE FORCES!

This game is despicably good!

Roblox is home to quite a few games based on movies, TV shows, comics, etc., and **Despicable Forces!** is one of the best, with great design (you begin by escaping from a 1980s prison spaceship, with tasteless carpets and scout ships that look like Rubik's Cubes) and smooth gameplay that uses a speedrunning style similar to Sonic. The story line adds a lot to the game and makes this a different experience from your usual obby.

★ WIN IT!

If you complete all the stages in the quickest possible time, receiving an S badge for each one, you can unlock a secret Green Hill stage based on the level from *Sonic the Hedgehog*.

7 ESCAPE CANDYLAND

Be careful! Avoid the dangerous bubbles coming out of the taffy!

Forget *Candy Crush*, this game is the sweetest thing!

A great starter obby, **Escape CandyLand** has colorful, well-designed graphics and a nice learning curve. The early stages are very simple, but after stage 20, you reach the castle and things get a little more challenging! It's not too long, so if you're looking for something you can complete in one session, this is ideal.

★ WIN IT!

If you see arrows on the floor of the maze, they're not a trick—they will lead you toward the exit. Be warned, the maze is surprisingly long!

6 ESCAPE SCHOOL OBBY

At this school, it's laser beams and lava pits that are your biggest hurdles!

A really fun concept, wittily executed, the **Escape School Obby** requires you to escape a school. At a normal school, this would be tricky because of the teachers, but in this school, it's tricky because of the laser beams and lava pits. It's not a long game, with just twenty stages, but it's very satisfying to complete. Also, your avatar will be equipped with a really cool uniform, so it's worth playing just for that.

★ WIN IT!

You can find the vault code in the YouTube channel of creator Sploshy, but to save you time, it's 134567. But watch the videos, too; they're funny—especially the Obby Song.

5 FLOOD ESCAPE 2

Make sure you pay attention to what your pet is saying.

This obby has an extra dimension: There are floodwaters rising, and if you don't figure out how to get out of each area quickly, you'll drown!

The maps are impressively open, in contrast with the usual one-route-through design of obbys, and you need to think differently and quickly. Beating the levels and racking up XP is satisfying. And you can play in groups, too.

★ WIN IT!

This is a cooperative game—you're not competing against the other players, and you can help one another. If you're new to the game, watch what the others do and help out if you can!

4 MEGA FUN

Will you find a pot of gold at the end of the rainbow? Or just another stage?

Got time on your hands? Try the longest obby on Roblox, **Mega Fun**—it has over 2,000 stages, with new ones regularly added. It's a great introduction to obbys because the earlier stages are straightforward, and you get the satisfaction of racking up a few badges when you pass them. New players might prefer to check out the sequel, **Mega Fun 2**, which isn't as long as the original (yet) but is more refined. And frankly, with over 400 stages, it's got plenty to keep you going for some time.

★ WIN IT!

In **Mega Fun**, enter the code dizc0rd to get a free skip. In **Mega Fun 2**, enter the code mymistakeooops for a free skip. The game's creator, Bloxtun, regularly posts new codes on Twitter.

∃ OBSTACLE PARADISE

This brings a whole new meaning to "space hopper"!

This was always going to be a winner if it was done well—a hybrid of two favorite Roblox genres, obby and tycoon. The more time you spend in the game, the more money you acquire.

While you save up the money to build your dream obby, you can play on those created by other users—which gives it a social aspect most obbys lack. Above all, it's a chance to build an obby in the knowledge that other people will try it out!

★ WIN IT!

You get a cash bonus each time you complete an obby with a Win button, so it's worth doing more than just hanging around in the game waiting for your money to go up.

Speed is important, but what really slows you down is messing up your jumps . . .

The "speedrunning" subgenre involves racing through a level against the clock, and **Speed Run 4** is the classic example, taking you through different landscapes with jumps and pitfalls to complete. Each time you complete one of its 31 levels, you get a ruby, and you can return to the game repeatedly to get more rubies and beat your best times. Timing is crucial—so is memorizing the layout of each level. Watch out for level 27—it's a killer!

★ **WIN IT!**

There's a tricky shortcut on level 14—if you leap across to the sloping tower on the right, near the beginning of the level, it's possible to scoot up it by hammering the space bar. Hold W to stop yourself from sliding back, and try jumping across to the next tower!

1 THE IMPOSSIBLE OBBY

SOME BRICKS CAN FADE

You'll need to keep your wits about you for this super-challenging obby.

This is an obby in the classic style, but it's majorly challenging! Its look and gameplay are simple—where other obbys are a riot of color and shapes, **The Impossible Obby** is cool black and pink neon—but it's got some of the trickiest stages you'll find anywhere. Unlike some obbys, your progress saves, so you can tackle the challenge in stages. The messages that pop up when you die add some extra fun, which is just as well because you'll die a *lot*.

★ WIN IT!

Hitting Shift locks the camera to the direction your avatar's facing. This is often useful in obbys, but in the more difficult ones like this, it can really help with those last-minute changes of direction!

33

? QUIZ

It's time to test your obby smarts . . . Do you have what it takes to win?

1

What is "obby" short for?

4

Which famous console game inspired the secret level in **Minions: Despicable Forces**?

6

Can you save your challenge progress in **The Impossible Obby**?

> I AM OBBY-VIOUSLY AN OBBY EXPERT! PLUS, I HAVE GREAT HAIR.

2

What do Roblox gamers call a jump where you have to go around a wall?

3

How can you tell if a wall is hoppable?

5

After which stage do you reach the castle in **Escape CandyLand**?

7

What's the longest obby on Roblox?

8

How many levels does **Speed Run 4** have?

 **⁇ ANSWERS** on pages 142–143

▶ BATTLE GAMES

There are many different types of battle games—you'll see categories on Roblox like FPS, Fighting, and Military. But there's often a lot of crossover between genres, and combat can take different forms.

Battle games are the most popular genre with creators—nearly two-thirds of Roblox games are battle games! But that's a lot of games to find your way around, so allow us to guide you to the best.

THE WORLD OF BATTLE GAMES

Let us take you through the main types of battle games . . .

BATTLE ROYALE

A number of players are dropped into a map and fight. Traditionally, the **last one standing** is the winner, but in a **solo deathmatch,** players can respawn after being taken out. They can rejoin the fray, and the winner is the player with the highest score. You can also have a **team deathmatch,** where you work together to score more takedowns than the other team.

WARFARE

Military-style games typically make more use of hardware, such as tanks. This includes larger-scale strategy games where you take control of whole armies or countries.

TOWER BATTLES

Defend a tower from some invading horde, such as zombies. The aim is to hold out as long as you can, usually competing against other teams who are trying to defend their own towers.

ONE-ON-ONE

This is a classic beat-'em-up style fighting game, in which you take on one other player and try to beat them in combat. Special powers and moves are crucial to success.

★ NOOB TIPS

HERE ARE OUR TOP TIPS FOR TACKLING BATTLE GAMES . . .

It can be annoying when you get into a battle game, and there are lots of other, more experienced players who target and take you out in the first few seconds of each round. Here's some general advice for new players.

1 Don't worry too much about winning the first few times you play. Instead, concentrate on exploring the map, so you know your way around.

2 Often, the hardened veterans will have a much better toolbox than you, either because they've earned it through playing or they've bought it with Robux. Be careful about getting drawn into games where you need to spend huge amounts of Robux just to compete!

3 Battle games need quick reactions, so your control setup can make a big difference. Moving, jumping, and using your weapon all at the same time isn't easy on a keyboard. Switching to Xbox, or using a console-style controller with your PC, may help.

DON'T WORRY ABOUT LOOKING LIKE A NOOB. JUST MOVE ON TO THE NEXT GAME—NO ONE WILL REMEMBER YOUR NOOBISHNESS!

Taking a swipe!

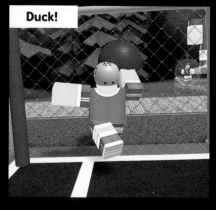

Duck!

Building for victory

BATTLE GAMES

To come up with this list, we dropped every battle game on Roblox onto an island and made them all battle it out. The winner might surprise you . . .

10 ISLAND ROYALE

It's no time to relax on the beach or go for a swim!

Yes, it's a *Fortnite* clone, even down to the flying bus you drop from after you spawn— but it's a really good *Fortnite* clone, with well-designed maps and smooth action. If you've played *Fortnite*, many of the same tactics will serve you well—high ground and moving with caution—and it takes a little practice not to get picked off easily. But it's a great feeling when you get good at it.

★ WIN IT!

Wait before exiting the bus—it can be dull watching it fly around, but it means that you can let some of the other players kill each other off before you join the fray.

9 DODGEBALL!

Dodge, throw, run, repeat—this will be the secret of your success.

You could say that this is technically a sports game, but only if you believe dodgeball is a sport rather than a form of school-approved violence. **Dodgeball!** works like its real-life equivalent: Two teams, each on their own half of the court, hurl balls at each other. If you get hit four times, you're out of the game. The first team to lose all their players loses the match. It's the simplest of games, and there's not much depth to it, but it's great for a quick blast and to play against friends.

★ WIN IT!

If you're getting hit out of the game too quickly, try sticking close to the fence. Bounce your balls off it toward the other team!

8 ZUMBIE ATTACK

Rule 1 of the zombie apocalypse: The zombies never stop coming . . .

Face off against waves of zombies and other monsters in this survival game. You start with just a basic pistol and knife, but you can upgrade using the cash you earn for takedowns. The difficulty level is nicely managed, with a hard mode that's only unlocked when you hit a certain XP—at first, you may find your character dies annoyingly quickly, but it won't be long before you get the hang of it! Be warned: This is one of the more horror-based games—though there's no blood.

★ WIN IT!

Stay on the move as much as you can—the zombies don't stop moving and can do a lot of damage to you while you're landing enough blows to beat them.

7 TOWER BATTLES

Those zombies may look small, but they can cause a lot of trouble . . .

This is a cross between a battle game and a mayor/tycoon game. You start off with one tower, in a land being attacked by zombies. The tower is your defense, and by keeping the zombies from passing through it, you'll get money to buy more towers. You can play on solo Survival mode or on Versus mode, where you try to survive longer than the opposing player. The different strategy options make this a rewarding experience if you stick with it.

★ WIN IT!

Towers that are also farms give you extra cash in the game—well worth getting so you can earn money while you fight.

Don't turn your back on the other towers for too long!

A simple team battle game, this puts players into four teams—blue, red, green, and yellow—and gives each of you a tower to defend and weapons to use. The towers are connected by bridges that meet in the middle, so you can choose to storm someone else's tower or defend your own. The winner is the last team left standing, even if their tower isn't. It's fast, frantic stuff and great for a quick hit of warfare—there's nothing like watching a tower fall after you've landed a direct hit!

★ WIN IT!

Shooting at opponents and towers with the bazooka is fun, but rebuilding your defenses using the wall function is an underrated tactic.

5 MURDER MYSTERY 2

Hey, what's that guy doing over there? Whatever, it's probably fine . . .

One of the most popular Roblox games, **Murder Mystery 2** plays very differently depending on what role you get randomly assigned at the beginning. The Murderer is there to take out others, and the Sheriff is there to stop them. In addition, ten players will be unarmed Innocents, who can help the Sheriff catch the Murderer by spying on them. You never quite know how a game will play out because different Murderers will tackle the game differently—so it stays fresh and keeps players coming back for more.

★ WIN IT!

Enter the code COMB4T2 to get a Combat II knife. Fresh codes are regularly posted on Twitter at @NikilisRBX.

45

4 BLOX HUNT

Table, book, or chair? Come out, come out, wherever you are!

This is hide-and-seek with an edge. Two Seekers and a bunch of Hiders are released into a map, with the Hiders getting a head start. The Hiders can click on objects in the map to disguise themselves as those objects. The Seekers must zap any objects they suspect might be Hiders—but the Hiders can zap back and put Seekers out of the game. The tactics of **Blox Hunt** make it super fun, and it can be surprisingly tense sitting on a desk disguised as a pile of books, hoping not to be found.

★ WIN IT!

The Summer Camp map has some dark corners that will hide you pretty well if you disguise yourself as a lamp, and it means that you'll see any Seekers coming.

③ BE A PARKOUR NINJA

Channel your inner ninja, and speed your way to success!

This game is loads of dumb fun. It's a battle royale in which you're all ninjas armed with swords, smoke bombs, throwing knives, and the ability to leap up walls like you're in a wuxia movie. The action is fast and furious as you all run at one another, swords swishing, and you can die incredibly quickly.

It's a great one to play with friends—you respawn fast and can go looking for revenge on whoever just got you.

★ WIN IT!

To run faster and jump higher, you can "climb" walls by running straight at them and pressing the space bar as many times as you can.

Things can get pretty tense in this first-person shooter game!

★ WIN IT!

Unusually for Roblox, **Phantom Forces** is an FPS (first-person shooter). It's a team-based battle game—you drop into a map and battle the other team. The environments are really impressive and well designed, with multiple floors, areas of cover, and vantage points.

Once you get the hang of the controls, it's loads of fun. Be warned, though—this is one of the bloodier Roblox games, and the first-person perspective pitches you straight into the action, so it may not be suitable for all.

Look at the map, and figure out where the spawn points are. It's especially useful to find out where the other team is going to spawn—depending on your strategy, you can attack or avoid them.

1 TINY TANKS

It looks just like playing with toys on the carpet IRL!

Perhaps the most ridiculously enjoyable game on Roblox, **Tiny Tanks** takes a similar style from the *Micro Machines* racing games and applies it to combat. From an overhead view, you take control of a toy tank and your team battles the other team.

There are four different modes— Deathmatch, Domination, Regicide, and Capture the Flag—and they're all great. The game is quick to pick up and offers a dose of non-gory violence.

★ WIN IT!

Always think about where your gun turret is pointing: When you're on the move, if you have nothing else to aim at, turn your gun in the direction you're heading, so you're ready if you run into enemies.

❓ QUIZ

Now you can fight for the quiz master title!

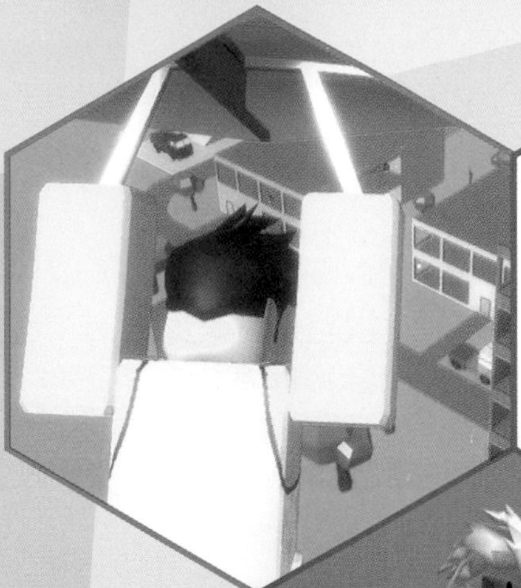

1

What are the three main types of gameplay in battle royale games?

4

What are the three different roles players are randomly assigned in **Murder Mystery 2**?

6

What AVK do you need to unlock the purple katana in **Be a Parkour Ninja**?

I'M A DODGER, NOT A FIGHTER . . . HONEST!

2

How many hits in **Dodgeball!** put you out of the game?

3

How many teams are there in **Doomspire Brickbattle**?

5

How many Seekers are selected at the start of a round of **Blox Hunt**?

7

What does FPS stand for?

8

Name two of the four modes in **Tiny Tanks**.

? **ANSWERS** on pages 142–143

▶ ADVENTURE

These games take you into different worlds and life-and-death situations, going beyond the everyday.

Whether you want to take on epic quests against fantastic beasts or dodge zombies in your own horror movie, this genre plunges you into every kind of drama you can imagine!

GAMES

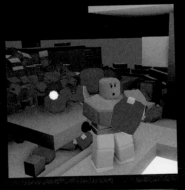

THE WORLD OF ADVENTURE GAMES

Adventure games can take a lot of different forms. Sometimes the gameplay area is huge, sometimes it's quite small; sometimes you're free to roam and do whatever you like, sometimes you have clearly directed missions.

SURVIVAL/HORROR

You're placed in a dangerous situation and have to get out alive. These games often have a smaller gameplay area, with a puzzle element—you must escape or survive the round—but they can be larger. **Apocalypse Rising** has the biggest maps you'll see on Roblox.

HARVESTING

In these games, you must find materials and craft and/or sell them in order to buy the items you need to progress. Often, this will be combined with another genre—you may need to buy items for combat, or there may be elements of a tycoon game.

EXPLORATION

Some games are just about exploring the game's world and give you a lot of space to wander around in. There's a lot of crossover between this type of game and a role-playing game.

NARRATIVE

A game such as **Heroes of Robloxia** is more like a traditional, Mario-style console game, with a series of missions that build up to a complete story.

Tough conditions

Epic battles

Watching out for trouble!

QUICK BLAST OR DEEP DIVE?

Because adventure games can be so different from one another, it's tricky to give general tips for playing them. When you start a new one, it's good to get an idea of how quickly the game's expected to go. Some of these are really short—you can play a few rounds of **Natural Disaster Survival** in a few minutes. Some need much more involvement—**Tradewinds** can take up hours and hours of your time. Choose a game that suits the way you like to play.

BREAKING OUT OF JAIL—AND BREAKING RECORDS!

FACT BOX

Jailbreak is the fastest-growing game Roblox has ever had, racking up more than two billion visits in its first two years.

ADVENTURE GAMES

Come with us now, on an epic quest to discover the very best in Roblox adventuring . . .

10 FLEE THE FACILITY

You need to reach "terminal velocity" to win this game!

In this survival game, you and four other players are dumped in an office building with long, winding corridors. There are computers scattered around the various rooms, and if you hack them all, you can open two exits. However, one of you will be randomly chosen to be the Beast, whose job is to keep the rest from getting out. It's fun, frantic stuff, with a good teamwork element—the more of you who stay alive, the more chance you have of hacking all the computers!

★ WIN IT!

On some of the darker maps, you can gain an advantage by switching to dark clothing. Also, the closets make good hiding places; many players never check them.

9 NATURAL DISASTER SURVIVAL

Dress for success—you don't want
to suffer a fashion disaster, too!

Disaster Warning:
Acid Rain! Stay indoors

An early hit for Roblox, this game has racked up
well over a billion plays since 2011. You're dumped
on an island with a group of other players, you get
about a minute to scope out the area, and then
you find out that a disaster is about to strike.

There are 11 different types, including earthquake,
tornado, meteor shower, tsunami, and even
a volcanic eruption. You just have to survive!
The combinations of different disasters and
maps make it compelling—and surprisingly tough!

★ WIN IT!

You'll know the acid rain disaster
is coming before the warning comes
up, because you'll hear a whistling
wind. Take cover!

After riding the normal elevator, you'll never look at an elevator the same way again.

This is the game in which you get into a seemingly normal elevator and ride up and down. Nothing out of the ordinary happens, and the doors definitely don't open onto a dance floor where you have to take part in a dance-off, or a park filled with dinosaurs, or a void where the elevator falls into nothing and you have to desperately try not to fall through the doors.

This is one of the weirdest minigame collections around, which is what makes it one of the best.

★ WIN IT!

When the elevator arrives at Jurassic Park, stay away from the doors if you don't want to get eaten!

7 HEROES OF ROBLOXIA

Live out your Marvel and DC fantasies with this game that allows you to roam around a cityscape, fighting crime and foiling villains. Although the world is extensive, the gameplay is quite directed—you accept missions (either with other players or going solo) and head off to complete them, using a combination of combat and puzzle-based gameplay. You get to switch between superheroes, so don't worry too much about what power you pick to start with.

 ★ WIN IT!

At the end of Mission 1, become Captain Roblox to deal with Cicada's minions, but switch to being Overdrive to fight Cicada himself.

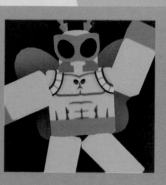

6 SHARD SEEKERS

This is where to find fantastic beasts!

Glittering shards are falling from the sky, and it's your job to collect them in this open-world game. If you gather enough shards, you can buy pets—and not just dogs, hamsters, and such: In this game, you can buy leopards! The extensive map, which has a *Legend of Zelda*-ish feel, looks great, and has so much to explore. Plus, it contains dragons that you can ride!

★ WIN IT!

The Skyhold floating islands not only give you a great view when looking for shards, you can also find a baby dragon there.

5 MOUNT OF THE GODS

WANT TO FEEL LIKE A GOD? BUY A VIP SERVER.
- SPAWN UNLIMITED ITEMS.
- PAUSE THE GODS.
- DESTROY YOUR FRIENDS WITH SPIDERS.
- HAVE EVERY MASK.
- ENABLE PVP.

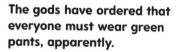

The gods have ordered that everyone must wear green pants, apparently.

This is a really original co-op game, in which players living on an island must do the usual things to survive—eat, drink, make tools—but also appease the gods by throwing items into a pit of lava. If you don't appease the gods, they become angry and burn down your forests or make you get hungry and thirsty quicker. The design is cute, and it's one of the funniest games on Roblox—even the tutorial and lobby are funny.

★ WIN IT!

If you equip the Mask of the Lumberjack and an axe, then go to a tree and press F and the left mouse button at the same time, you'll activate a glitch that supplies extra wood.

★ WIN IT!

You don't have to fight bosses alone—join forces with four or five other players, and you'll be able to take them down much quicker.

Here's a big fantasy game with lots of sword-slashing action. You start off with a basic sword and armor, tackling beasts in the woods to raise your XP, but before long you'll be upgrading your equipment, teleporting to other areas, and searching for bosses. There's loads of space to explore and rare items to track down—this is one to really sink some time into.

3 APOCALYPSE RISING

Gear up for the apocalypse—you're going to need to . . .

This survival horror game is noted for the scale of its maps—over 40,000 bricks. But it's not just big—it's the most realistic and detailed world you can imagine in Roblox. You drop into a map with a gun and a torch, then must try to avoid being killed by—you guessed it—zombies.

You need to keep an eye not only on your health but also on your hunger and thirst. It's great slow-burning stuff—really tense and atmospheric.

★ WIN IT!

Don't jump or sprint unless you really need to—you'll make noise and increase your hunger and thirst. Crouch to avoid being seen, and move silently.

63

2 TRADELANDS

Time to trade land for water as you head out on the high seas.

This classy game of adventure on the high seas takes you back to the eighteenth century and offers you the chance to play as a merchant or a pirate. It's got a *Minecraft*-style element where you must harvest materials and craft them in order to make ships and equipment. There's also lots of worlds to explore, where you can trade or steal, invite friends to join your crew, and even wage warfare against others. You can lose yourself in this game for days.

★ WIN IT!

Check the wind direction when sailing by looking at the little flag on top of your ship. You'll go faster sailing with the wind.

1 JAILBREAK

Don't worry, security at real prisons is *much* better than this.

The best open-world game on Roblox allows you to choose between playing as a cop or a criminal. If you choose criminal, you'll start off in jail, where you must steal a key, then dodge the cops and wardens to get out into the city, where you can get down to the serious business of stealing stuff. If you're a cop, it's up to you to catch the criminals. With a good variety of places to rob, **Jailbreak** strikes a great balance between clear goals and letting you do whatever you want, which is why people come back to play it over and over again.

★ WIN IT!

You'll need a key card to escape the prison, but killing a cop only gives a one-in-four chance that they'll drop one. Pickpocketing is more reliable.

Venture into these questions to test your game knowledge.

1

How quickly did **Jailbreak** reach two billion plays?

4

In **Shard Seekers**, what can you find on the Skyhold floating islands?

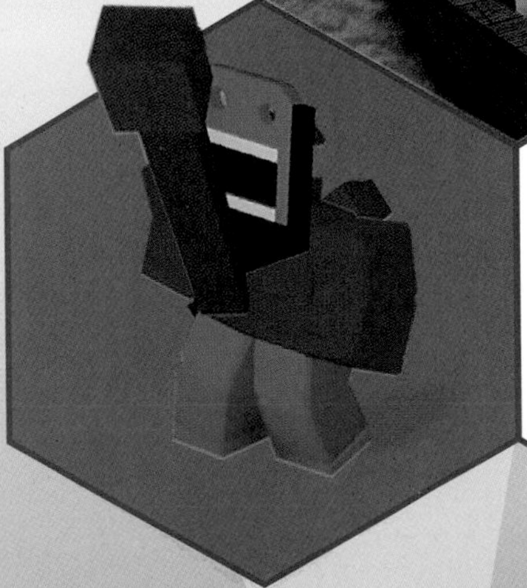

6

What are the two starter items in **Apocalypse Rising**?

AND SO, THE ADVENTURE GAMES CHAPTER ENDS . . .

2

How many different types of disasters are there in **Natural Disaster Survival**?

3

Do you have to face bosses alone in **Swordburst 2**?

5

What do the gods in **Mount of the Gods** burn down if you don't appease them?

7

What century is **Tradelands** set in?

8

What's the chance of a killed cop dropping a key card in **Jailbreak**?

❓ ANSWERS on pages 142–143

▶ TYCOON GAMES

Tycoons have become huge in the age of mobile gaming, so it's no surprise they've done well on Roblox, too.

You start off with some money, which you use to build things that will make more money, which you use to build things that will make more money, which you use . . . and so on and so on, until you become really, really rich—or lose all your money trying!

pizza prince noir

Thanks!
Ringing. . .
Hello?. . .

▶ THE WORLD OF TYCOONS

This genre includes some of the most creative games on Roblox, where the only limit is your imagination . . . and your money.

$35K

$100K

DROP IN

The simplest type of tycoon is a dropper-and-conveyor game. In these, you start with a machine that drops items onto a conveyor, which are sent off and earn you money.

These games tend to have little risk—the money keeps coming in whatever you do—and you don't get much choice about the layout of your factory/base, with each piece appearing in a fixed spot after you buy it.

To keep it interesting, these games often let you buy items that you can do other things with, such as vehicles for going to other places and weapons for battling other players.

TOP TIP!

Dropper-and-conveyor tycoons are pretty straightforward to put together—that's why there are a lot of them on Roblox!

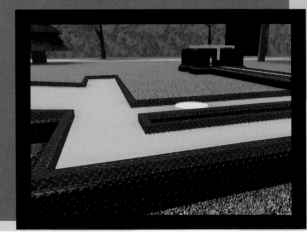

$15.7K
$5K

$13.5K

> SOMETIMES YOU HAVE TO SPEND MONEY TO MAKE MONEY . . .

$70.5K

FREE MARKET

Roblox also has a lot of sandbox tycoons. If you've ever played *Sim City*, these games are a lot like that. You get a plot of land or a basic unfurnished building, plus some starter money that you can choose to spend on a variety of items in a catalog. You're free to place your items wherever you like, so you can really make it your own.

Unlike with dropper-and-conveyor tycoons, where the dropper will keep making money, you need to make sure you spend your starter money on things that will make more money for you, or the game will be over before it starts! In **Retail Tycoon**, for instance, make sure you buy storage before you order supplies, or there'll be nowhere to put them—and you need a cash register so you can sell stuff.

Well-stocked shelves

Shopping trip

New investments

Sign
$200

Image sign
$430

$7.5K

TYCOON GAMES

Want to make lots of money?
Well, we can't help you there.
But these great games let you pretend.

10 LUMBER TYCOON 2

X: ← 2.2 →
Y: ↓ 2.2 ↑

Money *does* grow on trees.
But you have to cut them down first.

This game can be a little tedious at first: You play as a lumberjack, cutting down trees and selling the wood in order to build your own home and lumber operation. You start with $20 to buy a basic axe, and it is *really* basic: Chopping down one tree takes ages, and then (sigh) you have to chop it up small enough to put on the drop-off conveyor belt. But when you get going, this is a really engaging game with lots of scope to do your own thing.

★ WIN IT!

After you buy yourself a plot of land for $100, you can take the sign that marks it with your username at the drop-off and sell it for $400—enough for a vehicle.

9 SUPERHERO TYCOON

Sure you want to keep that spider in a glass case, Spidey?

You start off with a superpower production line, and the upgrades available as you accumulate cash mean that you can build your own superhero lair. You can choose to play as one of several DC and Marvel heroes (no female ones, though—where are Wonder Woman and Captain Marvel?) and work your way up to buying weapons and, most excitingly, a costume. This game is so popular that a lot of people have produced scams with similar names, so make sure that you get the right one!

★ WIN IT!

While waiting for your own money to build up, you can go over to other players' bases and stand on their cash terminal to stop them from collecting their own.

Cash to Collect:

$180

8 MINER'S HAVEN REINCARNATION

This mine is mine. If you want a mine, build your own.

This ambitious hybrid of the dropper and sandbox genres casts you as a miner with three iron droppers, conveyors, and other equipment. However, you have flexibility over your approach to the game, earning research points, building elaborate bases, and trying to climb the leaderboard.

There are loads of items to collect, giving this game much more depth than most tycoons.

★ WIN IT!

You can use timed droppers or remote droppers in this game. Remote droppers can earn you more, but you need to operate them yourself, whereas timed ones will work automatically.

7 WIZARD TYCOON

Hope you don't suffer from staff shortages in this game . . .

This is like being a supplier to one of the shops in Harry Potter's Diagon Alley. There are two versions of the game, a single-player and a two-player co-op, in which one of you takes the role of worker and the other is the owner. You set up a castle-style factory that makes potions and so on. Each arena has three other factories in it, and while you're waiting, you can go off and attack them if you like. It all looks awesome.

★ WIN IT!

It's worth saving up for the Meteor Staff—if other players come around hassling you, you can drop a load of meteors on them.

6 PIZZA FACTORY TYCOON

You'll want to get it while it's hot!

This is one of the best dropper tycoons because the game mechanics are so well worked out. In this game, you start with a pizza base maker, a conveyor, and an oven. Collect the pizzas to earn money, and you can buy machines to add toppings, as well as parts for your factory and shop.

The interactions with AI customers make you feel like part of a world—there's definitely more to this game than just collecting all of the items.

★ WIN IT!

Some combinations of toppings increase the value of the pizza. Four helpings of garlic make the For Vampire Slayers pizza, while tuna, salmon, prawns, and shrimp make a Sea Supreme.

5 AIRPORT TYCOON

Excellent design makes this an original take on the dropper-and-conveyor format. The conveyor is the one that takes your bags before you catch a flight, and the more bags that pass through your little island airport, the more money you can make.

The Hawaiian-style setting is blissfully relaxing, and when your airport is big enough for a plane to take off from it, you can fly and explore other islands.

★ WIN IT!

Click on the Twitter logo, and type in AIRPORT to receive 15,000 cash.

4 CLONE TYCOON 2

Rainbow

This game is basically all-out clone wars!

Why work when you can make clones of yourself and get them to do it? This game sets you up on another planet with nothing but a clone machine and a sword. Once your clones are made, they head out into the landscape to kill other clones and earn money. With the cash, you can set up a mining operation and build a pretty sweet space base.

It's not the most challenging tycoon— the clone machine is basically a dropper— but the setup is very cool.

★ WIN IT!

The game features two quests. Go to the observatory and look through the two telescopes. Each one is pointed at a planet. Use a vehicle to fly to these planets to access the quests.

3 RETAIL TYCOON

This store has everything!

Scanning for success!

Start off with a small, empty building, turn it into a convenience store—and from there, grow it into a vast retail emporium. The bigger it gets and the more money you make, the better items you can buy.

This game needs more attention than some tycoons—you need to watch your stock to make sure that you don't run out, and keep an eye out for robbers, too. It can get stressful, but it's also a lot of fun!

★ WIN IT!

It's really worth getting a manager for your store, because they order more stock automatically. But you don't need more than one!

I'd love the cheeseburger!

I've been meaning to taste the cheeseburger!

Remember, customers always prefer service with a smile!

This is similar to **Retail Tycoon**, except the aim—obviously—in **Restaurant Tycoon 2** is to build a successful restaurant. You choose from eight different national cuisines—Japanese, Chinese, Indian, Greek, Italian, British, American, and Mexican—and it's up to you to furnish your restaurant and hire staff. You can work in your own restaurant, which makes you feel really involved, and the game is packed with charm. New quests are added regularly.

★ WIN IT!

When you can afford it, get the Tip Jar upgrade and buy a tip jar from EKEA, the game's furniture store (first table on the right). Any resemblance to a real-life Scandinavian store is purely coincidental, we're sure!

1 THEME PARK TYCOON 2

What could be better than building your own theme park? This is a perfect tycoon—really simple to pick up, and really draws you in due to the way the rides get bigger and better the more money you make. You start off with fairly tame teacup rides and make your way toward designing your own roller coasters. What's great about this is that you can just enjoy building, or you can get into the details of micromanaging your park—it's up to you.

★ WIN IT!

If you want to get a five-star park, make sure things like stands, restrooms, and benches are evenly spread around, so guests don't have to walk too far. Scenery is important, too!

You need to be right on the money to answer these questions

1

What are the two main machines in the most basic type of tycoon?

4

How much money do you start with in **Lumber Tycoon 2**?

6

What's the garlic pizza called in **Pizza Factory Tycoon**?

LIFE IS A ROLLER COASTER WHEN YOU PLAY TYCOON GAMES!

2

What are the two roles in a two-player game of **Wizard Tycoon**?

3

How many female superheroes feature in **Super Hero Tycoon**?

5

What items go on the conveyor in **Airport Tycoon**?

7

How many telescopes are in the observatory in **Clone Tycoon 2**?

8

What's the furniture shop in **Restaurant Tycoon 2** called?

 **? ANSWERS** on pages 142–143

▶ ROLE-PLAYING

This category includes the most popular games on Roblox—you can live your best lives playing them.

These games let you live a different lifestyle, make your own home, try out jobs from the adult world—and hang out with your friends.

GAMES

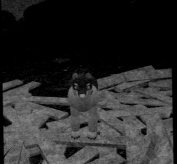

You look like the kind of chap who'd help a friend out!

Mind looking after this egg?

THE WORLD OF RPGS

Role-playing games, or RPGs, are perfectly suited to the online multiplayer gameplay of Roblox—you enter a world where the other characters aren't controlled by an AI but by other players.

REAL LIFE OR FANTASY?

RPGs are a little different in Roblox compared to RPGs on consoles or in tabletop gaming. Generally, RPGs in those areas are fantasy games like *Dungeons & Dragons* or *The Legend of Zelda*. But on Roblox, the games usually called RPGs are about going into a sandbox world to socialize—sometimes in a fantasy land but often in a real-world setting where you get to do real-world jobs.

You can customize your avatar and home, and the games often give you tasks to complete to earn in-game currency to spend on yourself.

PICK AN OCCUPATION!

There are simulators of activities like driving a train or plane, or being a vet—giving young gamers a chance to play at doing a grown-up job. (But trust us, it's more fun than doing a real grown-up job.) One of the most popular games, **Work at a Pizza Place**, is about . . . well, you figure it out.

JUST HANGIN'

The social side of these games makes them hugely popular—players use them like a social network, hanging out to chat with their friends. That's why they rack up so many visits—these aren't games you "win" or "complete"; they're games you keep dropping into.

However, this also makes RPGs open to those who want to harass others: They'll crash other people's parties or activities and start hassling them. So be ready to report anyone who's behaving badly.

TOP TEN

ROLE-PLAYING GAMES

This genre includes some of the most-played games on Roblox, so getting it down to the top ten was really tough! But it does show how amazingly different these games can be—from open worlds where you can go anywhere and do what you like to simulators of jobs and activities, to games that take you to fantasy worlds.

10 NEVERLAND LAGOON

Doesn't everyone want to pretend to be on an island paradise?

This game is so popular, it's spawned its own range of toys! It's an open-world game set in a land of mermaids and pirates. You design an avatar, for which you can acquire new items—and then just explore the world. The scale of it is impressive, but players who enjoy the social side will probably get the most out of it—a lot of the fun is in creating your avatar and then showing it off.

★ WIN IT!

There's a secret VIP room filled with clothes, accessories, and special abilities—when you start the game, walk into the throne room and through the dark doorway to the left of the thrones.

9 ADOPT ME!

I feel sick . . . let's go to the hospital.

Pay attention to what your pet is saying.

Pet Shop

The aim of this cute city-life game is to hatch pets from eggs and then look after them— by feeding them, taking them to the hospital, doing fun things with them, and so on. Looking after your pets earns you money (if only real life worked like that!). It's simple to pick up but keeps you coming back with its regular rewards— and as you get more and more pets, you can trade with other players, making this one of the most fun social games on Roblox.

★ WIN IT!

You get cash rewards just for being online—so if you leave **Adopt Me!** open while you're doing other stuff, you can get extra money without doing anything!

Hear the call of the wild, and step into the wilderness.

In this game, you get to role-play *as* an animal, designing your own wolf avatar and roaming around forests and mountains. It's a very community-based game—you can join a pack and even take a job in the hospital or school.

It has a very handsome, distinctive look, quite different from other Roblox RPGs, and it really transports you away from your everyday life into a calmer, more tranquil world.

★ WIN IT!

If you want to claim a den, first you need to join the developer's group— Shyfoox Studios.

7 ROYALE HIGH

Enroll at a school like no other!

After a hard day at school, why not unwind by . . . going to school? **Royale High** offers the fantasy high school of your dreams, where you can attend classes in the daytime and socialize in the evening—and unlike in real life, schoolwork earns you diamonds that you can use to buy items. With a relaxed pace, this is a game where you can hang out and explore the world. Watch out for the chat here, though, it can get a *little* aggressive.

★ **WIN IT!**

Sunset Island is a great place to explore—it contains two chests with accessories and a third containing 250 diamonds.

6 KINGDOM LIFE II

**Nice evening for a stroll around
the kingdom . . .**

This RPG takes place in a world more
like many standard RPGs found on
consoles: a medieval land of castles,
knights, and wizards. The original
version was discontinued, but a revival
created by DevBuckette has racked up
50 million visits.

There are so many options here—you
can go on quests, mix potions, even
choose to play as an elf, ghost, or orc.
It looks awesome, with lots of different
environments and atmospheric corners.

★ WIN IT!

If you want some guidance on what
to do to make the most of this game,
join the **Kingdom Life II** group, which
regularly organizes group role-play.

5 WELCOME TO BLOXBURG

This costs 25 Robux to access and is one of the few paid-access games on Roblox to become really popular. Which of course means you can't play it to find out if you like it before you buy it—but if you've ever played *The Sims*, you'll have a decent idea. As well as the usual RPG activity of customizing your house, you must boost your character's mood, explore the city, look for a job, or teach yourself new skills. It's easy to get really invested in your character's life!

★ WIN IT!

The highest-paying job is pizza delivery driver, but there's a downside—orders can come from anywhere on the map, which sometimes means a long trip.

Dino-life isn't easy, so make some friends and be part of the herd.

Who wouldn't want to play at being a dinosaur? In this, you can choose to play as one of several different dinosaurs, each with different characteristics (some are carnivores, some herbivores).

It's got a social aspect—you can choose to form a herd with others—but the aim of the game is survival, with threats coming from predators, hunger, and harsh weather. It's not as easy as it sounds—this isn't a hang-out-and-chill type of RPG!

★ WIN IT!

If you're a small water-based dinosaur, and you're attacked while underwater, find a hole that'll let you go underneath the island. Your attacker won't be able to follow.

3 FASHION FAMOUS

Pick your clothes, and strike a pose!

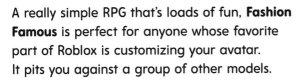

A really simple RPG that's loads of fun, **Fashion Famous** is perfect for anyone whose favorite part of Roblox is customizing your avatar. It pits you against a group of other models.

You start off as an Amateur Model, you're dropped into a huge walk-in closet, and you have limited time to assemble an outfit for yourself. When the time's up, you head out onto the catwalk and rate other peoples' looks. The look with the highest score wins. The different categories add variety, and there are so many items to explore.

⭐ WIN IT!

Hats and hair are really important—people tend to look at the head first, so make sure it looks good!

2 WORK AT A PIZZA PLACE

Is that pizza chef wielding a pizza wheel or a sword?!

The supersmart thing about **Work at a Pizza Place** is how it combines the social aspects of RPGs (the money you earn at the pizza place can be spent on your home and avatar) with a sense of progress as you take on the different jobs available: delivery driver, supplier, pizza boxer, cashier, cook, and manager. One of the oldest games on Roblox, this is still a strong favorite because the cooperative gameplay is so strong—if you don't all do your jobs properly, none of you make money.

★ WIN IT!

When you're a cook, make sure the pizzas don't end up on the floor— they'll attract bugs. Eeeewww!

1 MEEPCITY

The most popular game on Roblox, with well over six billion visits, **MeepCity** smoothly combines several Roblox genres. The core of it is a social town-and-city game, similar to *Club Penguin*, where you adopt a pet called a Meep (a colored ball with eyes) and customize your home. But to do this, you'll need coins—which you can get by fishing and selling what you catch, selling flowers, or playing games. There's a great Meep-based, Mario Kart–style obby game: **Meep City Racing**. With so much to do, it's no surprise that players keep coming back for more.

★ WIN IT!

When fishing on the dock, there are three boards underneath your avatar. The best time to release when casting your line is when the arrow is over the middle board.

❓ QUIZ

Now's your chance to role-play as a quiz-winning champ!

1

Where does your pet come from in **Adopt Me!**?

4

Who created the revival of **Kingdom Life II**?

6

What level do you start off at in **Fashion Famous**?

I CAN MAKE PIZZA ONE DAY AND BE IN A FASHION SHOW THE NEXT!

2

What's the name of the developer in **Wolves Life 3**?

3

Where can you find 250 diamonds in **Royale High**?

5

How many Robux do you have to pay to play **Welcome to Bloxburg**?

7

Name three of the six jobs you can do in **Work at a Pizza Place**.

8

What two items can you sell in **MeepCity**?

? ANSWERS on pages 142–143

▶ MAKING GAMES

What makes Roblox really different from other platforms is the ability to make your own games.

If you're not satisfied with just playing and want to be a Roblox developer—read on!

▶ THE BASICS

First, you need to download and install Roblox Studio, which is available for PC and Mac. (It's too complicated to design games on a phone, tablet, or Xbox—you need a keyboard—so the Studio isn't available for them.) The Studio can use up a lot of system resources, so the more powerful a system you can use, the better.

MODELS

You can make any kind of game in Roblox—anyone who's spent time playing games on the platform will know that. But different types of games need different skills, and it can take a while to learn those skills. That's why it's a really good thing that Roblox Studio comes with seven gameplay presets, where stuff like the shape of the play area and the mechanics are already figured out for you. This means that you can get started really quickly.

Racing: A car-based racing game.

Obby: The classic floating-in-a-void obby style.

Line Runner: A different kind of obby, with a side-scrolling view. The player runs continuously and must dodge obstacles as they go.

Infinite Runner: This is another continuous-running obby, but it is viewed from behind.

Capture the Flag: A battle game in which teams compete to capture one another's flag.

Go for Castle . . .

. . . or Western . . .

PLACES

You will also find a set of Theme templates. These give you a basic world that you can customize using a popular style of setting—Village, Castle, Suburban, Pirate Island, Western, City, and Starting Place. Starting Place contains a construction yard and is like a tutorial for designing different environments.

Team/FFA Arena: The basic battle format—you can choose to fight in teams, or solo (FFA stands for Free For All).

Combat: A battle royale–style game where players must race to grab weapons and start fighting.

CUSTOMIZE YOUR TEMPLATE TO CREATE A GAME THAT'S TOTALLY UNIQUE.

Start/Finish

. . . or Racing!

▶ HOME MENU

There's a lot going on in Roblox Studio, so let's look at some of the main functions in the Home menu.

CLIPBOARD

Lets you cut, copy, and paste objects, just like you would if you were typing something out.

TERRAIN

Options for reshaping the land, like changing its color, raising it, lowering it, and flattening it.

INSERT

Lets you put objects into your landscape. This is extremely useful! Toolbox opens a window full of premade objects, and you can search for what you need. This saves lots of time. If you want to make your own objects, you can use Part to get basic shapes that you can put together.

TOOLS

Here you can select, move, rotate, and change the size of objects. You can also set collision, which means you can decide whether two objects are allowed to overlap. For instance, if you set collision on a wall to "off," a character will be able to walk through it.

TEST

Play your game to see how it's working.

TOP TIP!

Set the **Toolbox** search to **"Ratings"** instead of "Relevance"—you'll find better stuff!

What's New ⑦ ⤸ Renbo9 ›

EDIT

Lets you change things like the color and material of objects. It's very helpful in making a game look like it's your own when you're using premade objects from the Toolbox. You can also Group objects (so that they stay together when you move them) or Anchor them (so that they don't move at all).

WHAT ELSE?

Most of the options you'll need are on the Home menu. But if you want to get more advanced, check out the other menus.

Model has options for changing the gameplay and adding scripts.

Terrain has extra options that aren't on the Terrain menu on Home.

Test lets you do things like multiplayer testing and seeing how your game looks on a phone or tablet.

View lets you add or remove things on the toolbar, and also contains some really helpful tutorials!

Plugins lets you add extra functions. You can search for plugins in the Toolbox—use the drop-down menu.

Explorer ⊡ ×

Filter workspace (Ctrl+Shift+X)

- 4-Way Intersection All-Way Boulev
- 4-Way Intersection All-Way Boulev
- Boulevard to City Street
- Car
- Model
- Model
- Model
- Model
- Model
- Model
- Model
- Model
- Model
- Model
- Model
- Model
- Model
- Model
- Model
- Model
- Model
- Model
- Model
- Model
- Model
- Model
- Model
- Model
- Model
- Model
- Model
- Model
- Model
- Model
- Model
- Straight Boulevard
- Straight Boulevard
- Straight Boulevard
- Straight Boulevard
- Straight Boulevard
- Straight Boulevard

✖ BUILDING YOUR FIRST GAME

Here's our step-by-step guide to making a runner game.

Drop in obstacles, such as . . .

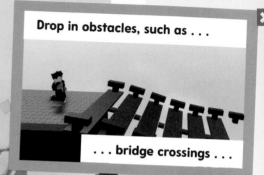

. . . bridge crossings . . .

. . . drooling zombies . . .

There are two types of running games in the Roblox Studio templates: Line Runner and Infinite Runner. Even if you've never played an Infinite Runner game in Roblox, you might have seen one somewhere else—*Temple Run* is the most famous example. In these games, your avatar automatically runs along a path, and you have to dodge obstacles and pick up bonuses.

. . . and trampolines!

We're going to start by building a Line Runner. The main difference from Infinite Runner is that you view the action from the side rather than from behind your avatar.

1

Fire up Roblox Studio, and select the Line Runner template from the gameplay menu. You'll see a baseplate* with nine different segments on it—you'll notice they're not connected.

> * BASEPLATE: A BASEPLATE IS THE "FLOOR" OF YOUR GAME, WHICH YOU BUILD ON TOP OF.

2

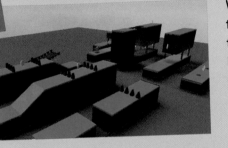

When someone plays the game, these nine segments will be put together randomly to make an infinite track. You can customize each of the nine segments to make the track your own.

> CALLING ALL ROBLOX FANS!

3

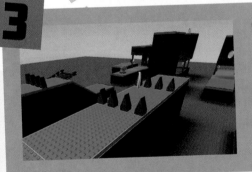

Click on any surface, and you'll see a list of its properties. You can change the material and color here. Try changing one of the surfaces to ice or neon.

4

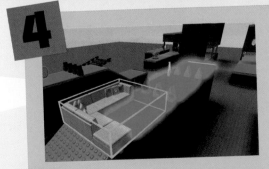

The Toolbox contains lots of premade objects. You can find something that would make a good obstacle—we thought a premium couch would be fun to jump over.

5

You can also insert NPCs, giving the player a moving obstacle to dodge. The drooling zombie works well in Line Runner.

6

When you've finished tinkering, click Play to try your game out. This is an important—and fun!—part of game design. Make sure it plays smoothly, the difficulty level is right, and it looks good.

7

If you want to change anything, just click Stop to go back to the studio window. When you're done, playtest it again!

IT'S AS SIMPLE AS THAT. HERE'S WHAT TO DO NEXT . . .

And that's it—your first Roblox game!

You can give it a name and upload it to Roblox for your friends to play, if you like. But don't forget to go on the File menu so you can save it to your computer!

TOP TIP!

If you mess anything up, the **Undo button** is your friend! It's the arrow at the top left of the screen. Next to it is the **Redo button**.

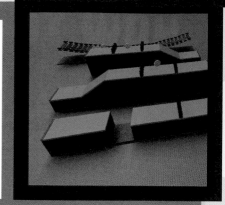

MAKE IT UNIQUE

Making a Line Runner is a great way to get the hang of customizing a game and making it your own. Because the gameplay is fixed—any Line Runner you make will work the same way as anyone else's. But the obstacles you add and how you change the environment can make it different.

Working with the Toolbox is a great way to speed up making a game. For example, it's much quicker to find a house in the Toolbox than it is to make your own using the Part menu to put together walls and decorate them. But the problem is that your game will probably look like a lot of other games on Roblox.

Customizing the objects from the Toolbox is a smart move. It doesn't take as long as making objects from scratch, but it changes the way your game looks.

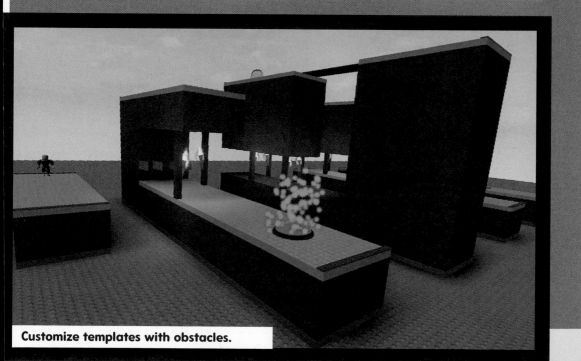

Customize templates with obstacles.

▶ HOW TO BUILD AN OBBY

Now let's try building a game that you can customize a little more. An obby is perfect for this because you don't need to worry about how the gameplay works—the player just needs to get past the obstacles without dying or falling.

1 Select the Obby option in Templates. An obby layout will load up, floating in a void.

2 Usually, you'd start building things before playtesting a game. But here, some of the work has been done for you, so hit **Play** and see what's in this obby.

3 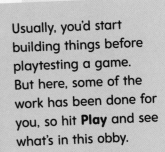 There are floating platforms to jump between and deadly red blocks to avoid. Along the way are spawn points—if you die, you'll respawn on the last spawn point you reached. At the moment, the game works . . . but it's pretty boring.

4

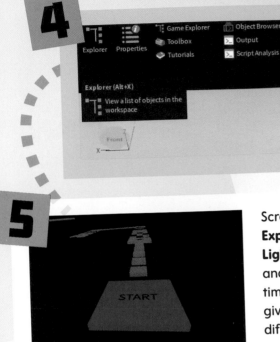

Now go out of test mode. Let's start by playing around with how your game looks. Click **View** and open the **Explorer** window.*

* IF IT'S NOT OPEN ALREADY, CLICK THE PROPERTIES BUTTON.

5

Scroll down in the **Explorer** window to the **Lighting** option. Open it and try changing the time of day. This can give your obby a different look.

* CHANGE TIME IN THE PROPERTIES LIGHTING PANEL.

6

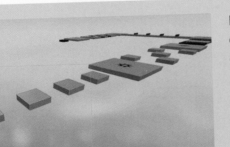

Now change the textures and colors. Left-click on a blank part of sky, and drag over a group of gray platforms. Make sure you don't select any deadly red blocks!

* TEXTURES AND COLORS CAN BE FOUND HERE.

7

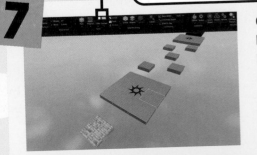

Change the texture and color* however you like. We went for a yellow brick road! By selecting all of your other safe blocks, you can apply these colors and textures to all of them. (Hold down Control as you click on the blocks to select a group.)

8

You can also change the color of your deadly blocks—we chose pink. (The **Appearance** box on the right of the screen lets you access a bigger range of colors.)

9

* MOVE, SCALE, AND ROTATE CAN BE FOUND IN THE HOME TAB.

Now let's try changing the layout. Click on one of the safe blocks at the beginning, then click **Move.*** You can click on the different colored arrows to drag it around the map. Make the layout trickier.

10

Try replacing one of the safe blocks with something else.

Select a safe block and delete it from the map.

11

Use the **Part** menu to drop a sphere onto your map where the safe block was. Change its color and texture. And when you are happy with its position, make sure it's anchored! Otherwise, when the obby starts, it'll fall into space.

12

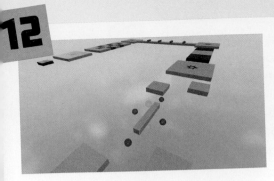

Make as many changes to the obby as you like. Here's a suggestion: Click on the safe block in the middle of the second section of the obby. Click **Scale** and make it really narrow.

13

Click **Move** and connect your narrow block to the first platform on the left.

14

Highlight the narrow block, and use **Duplicate*** to make more of them. They will appear in a stack next to the first one.

> ***DUPLICATE CAN BE FOUND IN THE HOME TAB ON THE FAR LEFT OR BY HOLDING CONTROL AND D.***

15

Move the narrow **blocks*** around to make a balance beam connecting the two safe blocks. You can make another balance beam connecting the other two.

> ***MOVE BLOCKS IF NEEDED.***

* GROUP BUTTON CAN BE FOUND HERE.

16

Try moving a spawn point using the **Grouping** tool. Select all the blocks that make up the spawn point platform, then click **Group.***

17

Now, when you select the spawn point platform, it will appear as a single item that you can move around the map. Once you're happy with the position of your spawn point, copy it.

18

Move to where the final spawn point is. Use **Paste** to create another spawn point platform, then position it a short distance from the final spawn point.

19

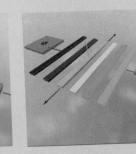

Fill the gap between the spawn points with obstacles of your own invention! Copy the safe and deadly blocks from elsewhere in the obby, and paste them here, or use **Toolbox** in the **Home** tab to find other objects.

* TYPE "OBBY" IN THE SEARCH TAB TO FIND THE RIGHT MODELS.

20

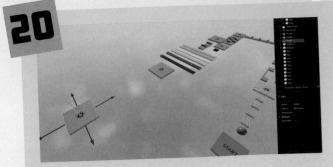

You can either stop here, or you can keep adding more stages.

Just remember to add a spawn point between each stage.

21

Playtest your obby. Make sure all of the pieces work like you want them to and that the difficulty level is right. Then go back and change it until you're happy!

The good thing about obbys is that you can keep adding to them if you have new ideas or discover a new object that you want to use.

You can also add a lobby. You've probably seen lobbies in other games on Roblox. Players will begin the game on your **Start** platform—so move it back, and then build your lobby around it. Or you can go into **Explorer**, click the plus sign next to **Workspace**, and click **SpawnLocation** to make a new starting point. Use **Parts** and/or objects from the **Toolbox** to build your lobby.

At the end of the obby, you can build a winner's room, so that players know they've completed it. More advanced designers can put prizes inside the winner's room for players to claim.

▶ HoW TO BUILD A RACING GAME

This isn't the most popular genre on Roblox, but building one is a great way to learn about making a game environment that works . . .

1

You can either use the Racing template or make your own game from scratch. First, let's try making one with the template.

Open up the Racing template in Roblox Studio. You should see four cars and four spawn points on a starting grid.

2

Again, because we're starting with a working game, it's a good idea to play it first. You can see how it works and get an idea of what you might change. So, click Play.

3

You won't be racing against anyone else, but take a spin around the track. The circuit takes you around an island.

4

Next, go out of playtesting mode. Before you change anything, let's take a look at how the game works. Make sure you have the Explorer window open (click it on the View menu, if not).

5

Click on the Start/Finish checkpoint. The Explorer window should go to a list of all the checkpoints in the race, with the first one highlighted.

6

Click on the arrow next to this first checkpoint. This should open a list of the checkpoint's properties, including two things called Finish and Start. These are **scripts**.*

> MAKE SURE YOU NEVER SKIP ANY CHECKPOINTS!

*****Scripts** make the game work. If you click on the other checkpoints, you'll see that they contain scripts called the Checkpoint. The game knows that a player has completed a lap after they pass through all the checkpoints and the Start/Finish checkpoint. If you skip any of the checkpoints, you won't complete the lap.

7  Click on one of the cars that's already on the grid. The Explorer window should go to a folder called Cars, which contains four objects marked Jeep. Click on the arrow next to Jeep, and this will open up a list of parts, as well as something called CarScript.

8 Scroll down the Explorer window until you find something called ServerScriptService. This should contain a script called RaceScript.

9  The script includes the messages that pop up on the screen during the race, so let's try making a little change that won't mess with the gameplay. Find the part that reads "Race Started!" and change it to something else, like "GO!" Be careful not to change ANYTHING except the words "Race Started!"

EXIT THE SCREEN BY CLICKING THE X.

We'll explain more about scripts later, because they're the most important part of making games. But for now, think about the layout of your racing game. Are there any shortcuts that players can take without missing a checkpoint?

10

Move to the stretch of road between the third checkpoint and the Start/Finish line. There's a bend in the road there that you don't need to follow—you can just cut across the grass.

11

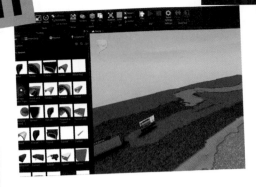

What could you do to stop players from taking that shortcut? Here's an idea: Search in the Toolbox for "tunnel."

12

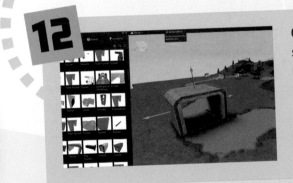

Choose a tunnel. Change the size so it fits the road, and move and rotate it, so that it's on the section of road that players can skip by cutting across the grass. Remember to anchor the tunnel, or it'll fall down when you start the game!

* TERRAIN CAN BE FOUND HERE.

13

We want to force players through that tunnel, so go over to the section of grass that they can use as a shortcut. Open the Terrain window.

14

There are lots of options for changing the terrain. Try using the Add and Grow tools to make a hill that players can't get through and must use the tunnel instead.

15

The Smooth option is useful for making your terrain look more natural. You can also go on Paint and choose a different material.

* THE PAINT TAB IS THE BEST ONE TO USE.

16

Another thing you can do to keep players from taking shortcuts is to add more checkpoints. Simply duplicate one of the checkpoints on the map . . .

17

. . . and put the new checkpoint wherever you like on the course. If it has the Checkpoint script, players will need to pass through it in order to complete a lap.

18

Make any other changes to textures and colors that make the game your own. Add anything you like from the Toolbox!

19

Some obvious things to change are the cars—you don't want all of the cars in a race to look the same! You can make them look rusty, metallic, plastic—even neon.

20

You can put any kind of car on the grid—but if you look for a cooler one in the Toolbox, make sure it works! Lots of them have been made for decoration, and aren't actually drivable.

21

Playtest your game. If you're not happy with it, go back and make more changes.

Ready to make your own racing game without using the template? Here's something you can try to make sure you've got the hang of how it works.

1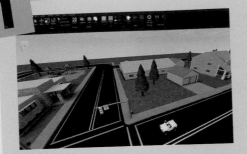

Open up the Suburban template. This is an environment without any game mechanics in it at all—but you'll notice that there are streets, a spawn point, and a jeep.

2

Now open a new Racing template. Go to ServerScriptService in the Explorer window, right-click on RaceScript, and copy it.

OPEN A NEW TEMPLATE. CLICK NEW OR SIMPLY CLICK ROBLOX STUDIO ON YOUR DESKTOP AGAIN TO CREATE ANOTHER TEMPLATE WHILE THE OTHER IS STILL OPEN. IT'S EASY TO SWAP BETWEEN THE TWO!

3

Go back to your Suburban game. Then go to ServerScriptService in this game's Explorer window, right-click on it, and paste RaceScript into it.

4

Now go back to your Racing template, and copy the Start/Finish checkpoint.

5

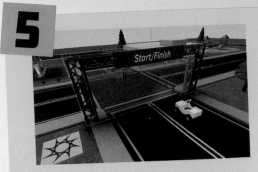

Paste a Start/Finish checkpoint into your Suburban game, next to where the jeep and spawn point are. (You'll need to copy and paste the stoplights in separately, since they're not part of the checkpoint!)

6

Copy a normal checkpoint from the Racing template, and paste that into your Suburban game, making a racing circuit out of the streets.

7

Duplicate the Suburban game's jeep and player spawn point three times each. Position these near the Start/Finish checkpoint.

8

Try it out! This should now work as a racing game, just like the one in the Racing template. If it works, you can either modify the Suburban template you have, or get a blank baseplate and start making a world of your own to play in.

▶ HoW TO BUILd A COMBAT GAME

Now we're ready to try something more complicated—a Combat game where we create our own objects and insert new scripts!

1

Open the Combat template. You'll see a baseplate in a void with a few objects on it. First, let's figure out how it works.

> ARE YOU COMBAT READY? LET'S DO THIS.

2

Take a look in the Explorer window. Near the top of the list of elements making up this game are four tools: AssaultRifle, ClassicSword, MedKit, and Pistol. Each of these items has a script that controls what it does.

3

Farther down, you will see SpawnLocation (the platforms where the players spawn) and EquipmentSpawner (the platforms in the middle). In the game, the tools spawn on these platforms, and the players can grab them.

4

First, we need some terrain. But if you build terrain over the baseplate, then all of the spawners will be buried. So, how do we avoid that?

5

Start by clicking on the Terrain option. The Terrain window will appear. Select Add.

6

Scroll down and you'll see options for Base Size and Height. Set the Base Size as large as it'll go, then set Height to 1.

TURN OFF THE LOCK, SO THAT SIZE AND HEIGHT DON'T MOVE TOGETHER.

7

Choose which material you want your terrain to be made from.

TOP TIP!

To make terrain quickly, go to Generate in the Terrain window. Change the variables, click Generate, and the Studio will make terrain for you—same as when you start a game of *Minecraft*.

8

Go to the map, and lay down some terrain. It should appear as a large flat block. Cover some more of the map, but make sure that you can still see at least one spawn point.

9

Zoom out and select the entire map. Now, when you click on any visible object, all of them will move. So, click on the spawner you've left visible, and move them all so they're on top of the terrain.

10

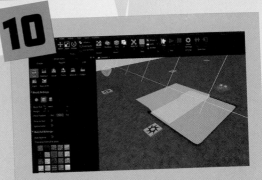

Now you can finish covering the map with terrain, filling in any gaps. Change the Base Size if you need a smaller chunk of terrain.

11 Move the spawners back into the middle of the map, where they were. Or move them wherever you like!

12

Now that you have a base layer of terrain, you can make changes to it—create hills, chunks of rock, and caves—or just leave it flat.

ALWAYS LOOK FOR WAYS TO KEEP YOUR GAME EXCITING!

13

Play the game to make sure that it works—it's a good idea to do that regularly, as you go along.

14

Decorate the map with objects from the Toolbox to make it interesting. This kind of game is more fun if there's stuff to hide behind and climb over, with different levels for going up and down. (Maybe try building your own structures with Parts.)

15

Give players some cool stuff to find—duplicate the item spawners, and put some more around the map, maybe in hard-to-find places.

16

Let's try building an object and putting a script into it. Click Part and generate a block.

17

Turn the block into a flat wall, and change the material to "Force Field." Choose a color for it—or leave it completely clear if you want players to be fooled by it!

18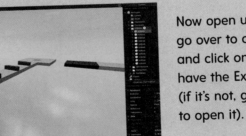

Now open up the Obby template, go over to one of the red blocks, and click on it. Make sure you have the Explorer window open (if it's not, go to the View menu to open it).

19

The Explorer window should be in a folder named Killbricks. These are the ones that kill the player when touched. Click on the arrow next to the Killbrick.

20

Right-click on Killscript, and open it. This script says that if something touches the block and that thing is a player, then the player's health goes down to zero—see the "0" at the end?

21

Copy the Killscript, and go back to your combat game. Select the Force Field, and it'll be highlighted as "Part" in the Explorer window. Paste the Killscript into this Part.

> DRAG THE KILLSCRIPT FILE INTO "PART." IT'S EASIER.

22

Decorate the map with objects. Generate some more blocks, then put them into position around your force field to create a frame for it. (There are some options on the Model menu that you may find useful here, including the Snap to Grid option.)

23

Make sure all parts of the force field and frame are anchored, then select them all and group them. (Make sure that you don't select any other objects along with them—just the ones you want to group.)

24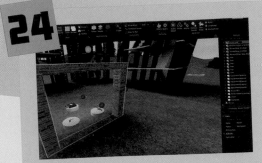

Your force field should now show up in the Explorer window as Model. If you like, you can change the name to something that identifies it better, such as "Death Gate."

25

Before you go any further, check to see if the Death Gate works! Click Play, go into the map, and run into the force field. Your character should die and fall to pieces. If it does, nice work! If not, check in the Explorer window that the Death Gate has the Killscript in it.

26

Now you can duplicate the Death Gate as many times as you like. Position them around the map.

27

Let's give your players something else to worry about! Search the Toolbox for "Drooling Zombie," and drop one into your map.

28

The Drooling Zombie should contain scripts to control its movement and behavior. Check that it's a Respawn script—if not, search the Toolbox for "Respawn script." Double-click and it'll be added to the Explorer window. Drag and drop it into the Drooling Zombie.

29

The Drooling Zombie will now spawn wherever you put it on the map—and when killed, it'll respawn in the same place! Duplicate it and add more Drooling Zombies.

30

Finally, you need a leaderboard to keep track of kills. There are lots of scripts for this in the Toolbox, but look for the official Roblox one.

31

Add the leaderboard into the Explorer window where it says ServerScriptService. And you're finished— it's time to try out your game!

▶ ADVANCED GAME MAKING

Ready to really sink your teeth into programming with Roblox? Here's a basic exploring game you can make to test your skills.

1 Open a baseplate, and generate some terrain.

> TRY IT AND SEE HOW MUCH YOU ALREADY KNOW . . .

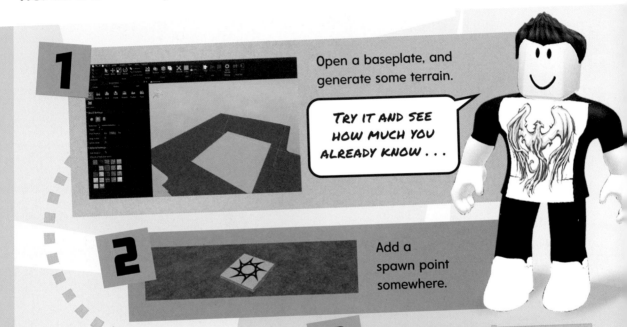

2 Add a spawn point somewhere.

SETTING A VALUE

3

What makes some objects in Roblox different from others? Why can you pick up some items but not others?

The answer is **values**. A value is a tag that you add to an object that lets it interact with other parts of the game in a particular way. So let's make an object and give it a value.

Don't use the Toolbox for this—make an object yourself using the Parts menu. It can be really simple—we made a sandwich.

4

Select the whole item and click Group. It will now appear as a model, rather than a bunch of parts.

5

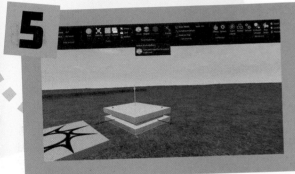

Now hold Control and click to highlight all the parts, then click Union to turn them into a single object. Rename your model—we've renamed ours "Sandwich"—and anchor it.

6

Click the plus sign on your model in the Explorer window, and you'll see a menu of things you can add into it. What you're looking for is a BoolValue. Add it to the model.

7

Rename the BoolValue "Scoopable."

8

Make sure that you have the Properties window open—if not, go to the View menu. In the Properties window, check the box next to Value.

So now that we've put this value into the object, what does it do?

Nothing, at the moment, because we don't have anything for the object to interact with yet.

WRITING A SCRIPT

Scripts are written in programming language—different systems use different languages, and Roblox uses one named Roblox Lua. It uses a combination of words, numbers, and symbols that give instructions to the game.

In a programming language, everything has to be exactly right. If you were writing a message to someone, you might accidentally type "funtcoin," and the receiver could probably guess that you meant to type "function." But computers don't guess. If you type something incorrectly in a script, the whole thing just won't work—even a capital letter can make all the difference.

Also, you need to make sure all your scripts are in the right place in the Explorer window. If you store a script in the wrong part of the game, Roblox won't know where to look for it.

IT'S ALL ABOUT LEARNING THE LINGO.

9

Download a **starter tool** from Roblox: **https://tinyurl.com/startertool**

Always remember where you saved it.

10

In the Explorer window, right-click on StarterPack and select Insert From File.

11

Insert the starter tool into the starter pack, and then rename it "scoop."

Playtest the game. You should now find that the player starts the game with the scoop. Like most Roblox tools, you press 1 to equip it and left-click to use it.

13

Go out of the playtest, and look at the Explorer window. Click on the plus sign next to the scoop (the tool, not the part that is also named Scoop), and look on the menu for Script.

14

IT REALLY IS PRETTY SIMPLE!

Add a script to your tool and rename it "ToolScript."

15

Open the ToolScript, and you should see this instruction.

```
print("Hello world!")
```

17

First, we need to make the scoop able to touch items, so type:

```
local tool = script.Parent
local scoop = tool.Scoop
local function onTouch
partTouched)
end
```

16

Delete it so the script is empty.

18

Then we want the scoop to actually do something when it touches an item, so let's add to that:

```
local tool = script.Parent
local scoop = tool.Scoop

local function onTouch(partTouched)

local Scoopable = partTouched.
Parent:FindFirstChild("Scoopable")
if Scoopable then
print("Scooped!")

end
end
```

This means that the scoop will look for the value "Scoopable," which we set up in our item. Because we checked the box, the scoop will know that the item is scoopable.

20

Now playtest the game again. Make sure that the Output window is open at the bottom.

19

Finally, add one line at the bottom:

```
local tool = script.Parent
local scoop = tool.Scoop

local function onTouch(partTouched)
local Scoopable = partTouched.
Parent:FindFirstChild("Scoopable")
if Scoopable then
print("Scooped!")

end
end

scoop.Touched:Connect(onTouch)
```

21

When you touch the sandwich with the scoop, the message "Scooped!" should appear in the Output window. If it does—**nice going!**

22 But just getting a message isn't very exciting, so let's make a counter to keep track of how many items you've collected. Go to the Explorer window, and find where it says ServerScriptService.

23 Make a new script in ServerScriptService, rename it "PlayerSetup," and open it. Delete the "Hello World!" thing again.

> LET'S MAKE THINGS A LITTLE MORE INTERESTING, SHALL WE?

24

Type this:

```
local function onPlayerJoin(player)
local leaderstats = Instance.new("Folder")
leaderstats.Name = "leaderstats"
leaderstats.Parent = player
end


game.Players.PlayerAdded:Connect(onPlayerJoin)
```

What we're doing here is telling the game that when a new player joins, it needs to put up a leaderboard entry for that player (it needs the "leaderstats" command for this).

25

Now add this into the script:

```
local function onPlayerJoin(player)
local leaderstats = Instance.
new("Folder")
leaderstats.Name = "leaderstats"
leaderstats.Parent = player

local items= Instance.new("IntValue")
items.Name = "Items"
items.Value = 0
items.Parent = leaderstats

local spaces = Instance.new("IntValue")
spaces.Name = "Spaces"
spaces.Value = 10
spaces.Parent = leaderstats

end
```

The "0" is important because it tells the game that you start with zero items. "Spaces" is how much space you have to carry items—we've set it at 10, but it can be anything.

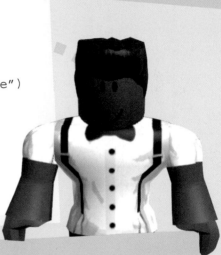

26

Playtest again and see if the leaderboard appears. If it does, success! But it won't go up when you scoop the sandwich—we need to add something to the scoop first.

27

Go out of the playtest, and return to the Explorer window. Open the ToolScript in the scoop.

28

THINGS ARE ABOUT TO GET MORE CHALLENGING. ARE YOU READY?

OK, now this is a little more complicated! Add this text into ToolScript:

```
local tool = script.Parent
local scoop = tool.Scoop

local backpack = tool.Parent
local player = backpack.Parent
local playerStats =
player:FindFirstChild("leaderstats")
local playerItems = playerStats:FindFirstChild("Items")
local playerSpaces =
playerStats:FindFirstChild("Spaces")

local function onTouch(partTouched)
local Scoopable = partTouched.
Parent:FindFirstChild("Scoopable")
if Scoopable then
if Scoopable.Value == true and playerItems.Value <
playerSpaces.Value then
playerItems.Value = playerItems.Value + 1
Scoopable.Value = false

partTouched.Transparency = 1
partTouched.CanCollide = false

end
end
end

scoop.Touched:Connect(onTouch)
```

JUST BE SURE YOU ADD ALL THIS TEXT INTO TOOLSCRIPT!

This means that when the scoop hits an item, it'll check whether you have space for more items. Then it'll make your items go up by 1, and the item will vanish.

29

Playtest the game to check that it works, then duplicate your object so you have ten of them. Hide them around the map.

30

You now have a simple exploring game! The player has to search for all ten items and collect them. When they've done this, they win the game. If you want to make it more challenging, try adding some Drooling Zombies for the player to dodge!

This is just a small taste of what you can do with scripts. You can make items reappear a few seconds after they've been harvested. You can make stores where you can sell items and buy upgrades. The more scripting you learn, the more you can do!

OBBY GAMES

P34

1. Obstacle

2. Wraparound

3. It has horizontal stripes

4. *Sonic the Hedgehog*

5. Stage 20

6. Yes

7. **Mega Fun Obby**

8. 31

BATTLE GAMES

P50

1. Last one standing, solo deathmatch, team deathmatch

2. Four

3. Four

4. Sheriff, Innocent, Murderer

5. Two

6. 50

7. First-person shooter

8. Deathmatch, Domination, Regicide, Capture the Flag

ADVENTURE GAMES

P66

1. Two years

2. 11

3. No

4. A baby dragon

5. Forests

6. Torch and gun

7. Eighteenth century

8. One in four

TYCOON GAMES

1. Dropper and conveyor

2. Owner and worker

3. None

4. $20

5. Bags

6. For Vampire Slayers

7. Two

8. EKEA

ROLE-PLAYING GAMES

1. An egg

2. Shyfoox Studios

3. Sunset Island

4. DevBuckette

5. 25

6. Amateur Model

7. Delivery driver, supplier, pizza boxer, cashier, cook, manager

8. Flowers and fish

GLOSSARY

CODE

The text that makes things happen in the game. Code is written in programming language, where particular words and symbols are instructions for the game to do certain things.

CRAFT

Make an item out of other items.

DEVELOPER

Someone who makes games.

GAME LOOP

A series of actions in a game where each action enables you to do the next action, eventually sending you back to the beginning.

GRAPHICS

The look of a game.

HARVEST

Collect items in a game that you can sell, craft, or use.

LEADERBOARD

A display in the game that keeps track of players' scores and resources.

MAP

The landscape a game happens in.

MINIGAME

A short, simple game found within another game.

NOOB

Someone who's new to a game and isn't very good at it yet.

NPC

Nonplayer character. A character controlled by the game itself.

SANDBOX

A type of game where there's no single aim, and the player is free to do what they want within the world.

SCRIPT

A piece of code that activates when certain things happen in the game.

SPAWN

How a player, character, or item arrives in the game. If something "respawns," that means it reappears in the game after being destroyed or used.

XP

Experience points—rewards in a game for completing tasks and performing actions.